The Invisible Season

The Invisible Season

Poems by

Nancy Andrews

Wayland Press
Indian Hills, Colorado

Grateful acknowledgment is made to the editors and publishers of the following periodicals and anthologies where several of these poems first appeared, some in earlier versions: *Ball State University Forum, The Bloomsbury Review, City Kite on a Wire: 38 Denver Poets* (Mesilla Press, 1986), *Colorado State Review, Communiqué* (Foothills Art Center), *Connecticut Poetry Review, Crossing the River: Poets of the Western United States* (Permanent Press, 1987), *December, Forum* (University of Houston), *Gold Dust: A Journal of Contemporary Poetry* (Sierra X-Press, 1986), *Hampden Sydney Poetry Review, The Kansas Quarterly, Kentucky Poetry Review, Muse, Roanoke Review, The Smith, Spree, Unitarian Universalist Newsletter, The Vanderbilt Poetry Review, The Villager,* and *Wisconsin Review.*

Acknowledgment is also made to the following for permission to reprint copyrighted material:

Harvard University Press: Epigraph from *A Poet's Journal* by George Seferis (translated by Athan Anagnostopoulos). Copyright © 1974 by the President and Fellows of Harvard College. Reprinted by permission of Harvard University Press.

Houghton Mifflin: Excerpt from "The Sonnets to Orpheus: Second Series, #12," from *The Duino Elegies and The Sonnets to Orpheus* by Rainer Maria Rilke, translated by A. Poulin, Jr. Copyright © 1975, 1976, 1977 by A. Poulin, Jr. Reprinted by permission of Houghton Mifflin Company. All rights reserved.

Special thanks to Carol Abel, Harriet Chase, Carol Christensen, and Charlotte Corbett for close reading of this book in manuscript.

Many thanks as well to our son Bradford for his encouragement and critiques, to Karen our daughter for her collograph (used for the cover of this book), and to my husband for his support.

—*Nancy Andrews*

Cover Art by Karen Andrews. Collograph reproduced courtesy of the artist.
Book Design and Production: Wayland Press, Indian Hills, Colorado.
Printed and Bound: McNaughton & Gunn, Inc., Lithographers, Saline, Michigan.

Library of Congress Card Number: 98-090331
ISBN: 0-933573-17-0

Printed in the United States of America
First Edition

for my family

CONTENTS

"And yet in the background is this pillar of light, this untouched thing that remains wedged in the heart of change like a diamond in a brook. There is a dreadful affirmation of one's whole being in such moments, like a Bach chorale, you think, that continues, irrevocably; *you know* that even if they suddenly machine-gunned instruments and musicians and listeners it would not stop."

—George Seferis,
A Poet's Journal: Days Of 1945-1951
Translated by Athan Anagnostopoulos

AND THERE IS RESONANCE

ADAGE

The evening pulled down its deep memory
Fastening into the hills with dark
Until the day was gone,
Evening clouds
Round in the rose were gone,
And comfort, like a dove
Settled under the dome.
The dome
Was speaking its silence
And the depth was more than equal
To fathoms of the sea
Where the
Whales were singing
Their ancient language,
Their adage,
Brain waves of a seventh world.

THERE, WHERE THE GROUND SWELLS

It came with pure cadence
strict as Latin, strong as ten Northern Oaks
inevitable as the rings that grow
however slowly at their centers . . .

cool lake of long glass without reflection
chalk line of solitude
stone
this silent architecture, a module
of my mother's death.

But I am among many energies—wind of her fire
opaque spirit
among layers of many crossings—intersectings
as birds dart
as drops of water intersect the sun
springing from the fountain
resonant as metal, incandescent.

There, where the ground swells,
the throated earth,
lies her determination
among the full roses.

I hear her,
the birds singing texts of triangles
through the morning breeze and wide acres.
Here,
stenciled on the perfect side
the perfect Nature of it,
is a morning of fresh speaking.

Death must be when the sky is invisible

but I see the sky—reach out my sight
looking for her
and sense filaments, in the blue light.

WHITE WALLS AT NOON

There is light through the long dust
    centuries of olive trees,
the air hums
beyond—the sea breeze scans
like a hand waving transparencies

long dust is humming a requiem,
the only sound.

White hours of noon pass idly
    in the village on the hill
going neither direction,
the streets are so narrow,
echoes have indelible shape

walls so white
    they are numb
stark judgments, standing there
challenging our color, startling
as a dark lizard on the sun . . .

we walk on the hum of cicadas
in the Greek noon light,

a labyrinth of streets
    sifting history
until we are white inside

carried on the hum of cicadas in the long dust,
the only sound.

Should a bell ring from the monastery
    on top of the hill
the white walls will break
with the sound

should the bell ring
    we will shatter
we will be white dust
in the Greek noon.

AT THE BORDER

Somewhere between Romania and Bulgaria
A Polish lady
Gave me hunks of bread
Portions of tea
To pass the night
Pouring her efforts into the droning.
I offered bits of vendor fare
Showed her pictures of my town
We forged one language
In between the steel wheels
Railing, clacking sound.

Officials,
Disbelieving passports
Slammed the sliding doors,
Decapitating sleep
Stood
Like ghosts in uniform
Under the dirty, swinging chandelier;
Drumming up a little paranoia
In the absolute night.

All the drama of the border
Was born in dismal station lights
Like a last stop
Before a land,
With no destination.

Then a cry outside the train
Drained me white
Cut my nerves in two
Pitched the night in deeper
Pierced with a question
Forever.

The Polish lady looked
As if she heard it every night
Until I saw her eyes
Go wild

And we were across the border.

LINES OF SUMMER, ASPEN

It is turning—thin sun, like a diamond key
all edges slightly inaccessible
the leaf so sharp
it is dozens of edges of silver.
A slight breeze is tracing these accumulations
and fine thin sounds of music
on white air . . .

exceptional profile.

A hummingbird calligraphs the air
between flowers   quick   selective
like tracing between points of wealth.

Such expensive surface between these trees
the flowers, well paid measurements,
the gold mosaic sun touches
this Medicean atmosphere;
a Ptolemaic sun
revolving around a town
centering earth.

THE AMA DIVERS

Many moons and Black Currents have flowed
In the history of the ama

The women dive
Harvesting the sea floor
Their long hair flowing
In the currents
Their whistling sounds
Haunt the waves,
Elegy of the sea.

There are prairies too
As vast as oceans
And thunder in hearts
That lie as deep and heavy
As water
Covered with stone.

The ama pry the abalone
From the deep sea rock
Like singly lifting stone
From a heart.

TRANSPOSITION

Principally, it is some great fortune
in these shadows of stone
moving
through a small dirt park in Tuscany.
These days are high fractures
of unbearable light
and bells
are striking centuries of resonance.

What does it mean
that quick radiance ahead
calling Christ
on this high broad threshold
the color of wheat.
Not one heavy foot is in this place
hear   not one Roman
stepping across its face.

Wait,
Romans stepped on the face of Christ.
See the tear,
great cresting of our frailties,
how they persist.

Here in this place
on a bench in a park,
deep in shadows of stone,
dark returning in light
and the light into marble
till the way the marble moves
is moving in us
till there is more and more light
luminous as the Florentine

and we see a painting of Christ,
the tear on His face.

That we should forget the sight of that tear—
Unthinkable.

Our tears are His,
don't we know this,
through all His resonance of centuries.

CHILDREN OF HONG KONG

Like two small silver fish
They jump from their boat to land
Textures of seaweed
Mixed with pocket coins

Flying into the plumage
Banners of laundry
Setting the city to sail.

Plied with parental errands
They weave in and out all nations
That scatter money and credit
Throughout the shops
Overflowing with boisterous wares

Where millions have a name
Demanding inch by inch
Sharing houses like tiny packages
With others
Who dip into the same dish
For some morsel
Of wrapped fish.

Do the children see at night
How the lights are marvelous stars
Swarming the steep hills
Sweeping down, puncturing the water
And the boats flick back to the hills.

Each night
The indelible stamp of their boat
Calls them
Planted by generations
Exceeding the amount of credit
Among all nations,
Floating there.

IN THIS STONE

A fine breeze
comes off these hills of Attica   moving
among the flowing sculptures of the heroes,
their free, translucent robes
barely knowing stone.

More power in the breath of blossoms
coming off these hills of Greece
than the high order of the waves
breaking on the coast of Amalfi

one walks through the echo of both.

Through these temples, these columns
a bird is singing.   It seems ancient,
metaphorical.
Hands of the statues—see how they touch
like song.

No Byzantine handiwork, golden boughs
tormented gongs around
nor complexities
in this flowing, simple stone;
these sculptures,
as if I could lay my eyes in theirs

and see forever peace
however distant   strong
those stone eyes stare.

PRE-DAWN ARRIVAL

The air is turning
earlier than dawn
steeples wait to spear the sun
I am waiting for time
to rise on this small French town.

A boy on a bike, wheels on the brick
throws long loaves
like morning papers.
I sit, composing more silence
hearing each thud of bread.

One shutter opens
on a second story window.
I think about night,
sometimes an anodyne
a cover of velour
or all night on the train
tasting gray.
I close both eyes
much like shutters.

I wonder what my friend will say
when day comes up with sun
having me here on the doorstep
along with the bread.

I am alone   in the hollow
that follows one sound.
If I could draw this shape
it would be my hieroglyph
in turning air.

A FACE FOREVER

How quickly
the train slides by on the face of Belgium
when you know
the ground is as deep as coal.

Like shadows we shuttle across
back and forth   sit down   get up   sit down,
each one writing a face like a hand
across the land.

Once in awhile
a face turns from its own shadow,
full
and takes over your life
blinding you with light

Like a halo on the cathedral
just outside
rising out of the ground, out of coal.

POINT IN THE ANDES

Now as you go out with this height
way out past the last chime
and all the people you are with
all of you
put your souls out there
one by one
and you look—seeing everything
in the nothing
the space is so great.

You all came
open-faced   wide-eyed
surprised
as if stepping off an invisible curb,
to take on the silence of stones;
if, on their way down
would never be heard striking
the canyon bottom.

And now
as if you had not had enough,
the Condors come, spanning,
carving blades into your souls
with some kind of dangerous wisdom
there where everything echoes
especially the cry of the guide
above   like a high priestess
announcing in omnipotent, gold-plated words

Condor . . . Condooor. . . .

So you place your mental offering
in sight of the black bird   who
pays no attention—curving away.
You have never been so satisfied
being so small   being paid no attention.
You have put all of yourself

outside
into space
into this heroic atmosphere.

TIBETAN COAT

This coat is like wearing a great territory
How I imagine those exotic
Extravagant earth places

A long horn
Blowing into the terror
The landscape

Brutal winds and small shrines
Prayer wheels swinging
Whirling

Nomads in stiff wool
In their tents
Sing plain songs
Embroidered with spiritual forces

Their deities hang hypnotic
On the slopes of Himalayas
Creating envelopes of safe keeping

Against the torque of mountains
Tearing the sky

My coat envelops me in stiff wool
Around me
I feel the great territory
Of nomad

DEEP TROPICS

It is dark with a violet moon
Hanging limp in the humid air
I lie back on the beach
Listening to Bach and Vivaldi.

Intruders
They and I
As I look out on musk water,
Seeing no end.

But this night takes me
Folds me on this shore
Repeats over and over
Soft reminders;
We all came from
Will go back to the sea.

This tropic was not meant
For this music.
Nor for the malarial white man
Who plays it for the visitors
Then slips out
With a beautiful Balinese woman
Who returns after a sensual pause
Slipping her health easily
Into flowers and dark water.
He returns much later
Looking malarial
And puts on another recording
Of Bach and Vivaldi.

BOAT MAN AT MOMBASA

He put on the day
The same as he had worn yesterday
On the early cool sand
He, an archetype
Whose print was on the tide
Stood
Pulling in his small, wooden boat.

A life of no illusions
Reduced to terms sharp as an edge
Routined, simple as a rock — practical
Everyday terms of line and fish and hook
Laid upon that rock.
It was likely
He patched his own sail
Most every day,
His dignity close
To the soul of the bone, the brine
The shell and the stone.

His day was always early.
He, wrapped in the gray morning mist
Went to wake the tourists
Sleeping under layers of their luxury
Before the day grew rounding.

They had been seized with the scene yesterday,
Wrapping it with their expensive
Surrealistic qualities,
Telling him
They would like to go out on his boat.

Now when he knocked on their door
He was struck deep
By the rude hard tone, like an auger,
Told to go away.

He could not smile all that day
As he had some hours before
When he said,

"Anybody go my boat?
We will get pretty beautiful shells
Out on the coral reef."

WHAT IS OUR PLACE

Across the sweep
The wide air spread
To each group of trees
Carefully placed
In the Imperial Garden Park.

A man wheeled a cart
Slowly
Into the frame.
He came in
Across the far distance
Silent
Yet moving his imprint
Like the mark of a tortoise
On the unblemished sand

As if to say,
"I am compelled to enter
All things."

A long gong in the distance
Sounded into the mind
Reminded . . .
One must whisper
Go on tiptoe
Through a Japanese Garden

Place the soul
Into the tree
Go only with the mind
Into the view.

SO TAKE IT NOW

. . . life is so full of beauty
beneath its covering
that you will find earth
but cloaks your heaven.
Courage then to claim it,
that is all.

— Fra Giovanni

In the outsweep of his arm
like an enormous wing,
I came to the rim
all this, all this now   before
after
over thousands of miles
the Great Rift Valley shimmered below.

An inversion of all choirs on earth
all the inverted roaring of the gods
was among the silence
honoring this ancient geology
the interminable patience of it
nothing could hear itself,
being so ancient;
that is when I knew I was dust
and the hearts of all the migrating animals
were dust.

On the shimmery African floor
coral pink flamingoes stood
fragile as iridescent bubbles touched,
like a breath . . gone
in an instant.

CORAL REEF

A thousand songs in porcelain air
Are there
To break upon the barrier
Fragile fragments — like color
Breaking crystal.
The shelves of coral and green
Deeper
And as clean
As the purest atmosphere
Protect lagoons they have made
Calm unusual aqua blue
From the thunder
Of the surf beyond.

AT KILAGUNI

In the African dusk,
A weight was thundering
But silence reached back in the dark thorn trees.
Soon
The Elephants came,
Single lines moving out, ears waving
Putting time down
In slow, enormous form.

They came down to the water to drink and bathe
Trunks swinging and tossing
Powdering with dust
To keep the flies away.

Long stands of contemplation — everlasting
Showed my rushing life absurd.

Then one by one to a rock,
Eternally the same,
They rubbed all sides
Then filed
Back to the bushes and trees.

I thought a ritual closed
But other long lines of them came
Out from the dark of those same trees.

Whose ritual?
We file every evening
to the veranda to watch.

UMBRELLAS AT 5:00 O'CLOCK IN MARIENPLATZ

The street was patent leather
Umbrellas wheeled like a giant Tilt-A-Whirl
Through a gauze of rain
Color swarming like bees,
An overlay of buzzing
The color against the gray,
Like some kind of immense conversation
Umbrellas moving every which way,
Each head hidden under a symmetric frame
Headless people scurrying in the rain
Under a melange of color
An expanse, almost undulating
Like a great Christo Project . .
Surely he has dreamed, covering Munich
With his surrealistic, bright eye.

THE NATIVES

The bray in the hills lasts longer than dust
In the village ground to bone.
Each day a mustard sun proceeds with the sage
To keep dry the countryside.
And a man strings beads in the dusk
Hoping an archangel will buy
At least let down a few cold tears.

We run with tinsel through this view
Admiring the glow of their native skins
Like bronze —
They live all days here.
Ah, that we could stay here we said
Be renegades
We said it on the note
Of an Andalusian guitar
Heard beyond the bray

And little do we realize.

IN THIS FIELD

A man bends like a crescent moon
to a field
bends to a wisp of a plant.
He is caved
like the flanks of a sacred animal
minimal, lean
a shadow in an empty, outside room; burning
under the great dry sky
for the monsoons have not yet blown
to fill the land's skull.
In this field he pours water from a jug
like a prayer
a thin, blue lens around the seedling.
He is long, dark
his space like a Brahmin   though shadow thin,
and there is resonance
between the man and his plant.
Down close to the ground there is sound,
the rhythm of growing things
and a moon   though a crescent
is a full moon
and would fit the space   the curve
where he caves and bends
like a Mandala is round with essence
no matter how the sky is
for growing things.

ONCE KNOWING A DREAM

Sometimes I see in the dark
The fantasy
I could not believe
The spires of gold leaf
Like losing my mind
To the middle of the sun.

Bangkok
Layers of silk and saffron stream
Across the electric bronze
Reality slants
As we look through amber glass
With a golden eye.

There is no extinguishing
The blaze of the Golden Buddha
Except
The Emerald One.

The earth is no longer difficult
Under that cool gaze.

UNDER THE AFRICAN SKY

The landscape has fine tuned
this space we have to imagine
we fit   with all Beasts
protracted into the first bone.

Coming here under this sky
in the giant system
of no margins
the sky scraping along the curve of earth
and any point whatsoever becomes resonant
                                        it is so alone.

Our first desire
is to wrap a cloak about us   as nothing
goes on and on
a thin wire slightly vibrating
                              and metallic.

Somewhere in the back, dark brain
there is this hammering
prehistoric   wild   and lost
and the clanging is ferocious

like something erotic or precious
the same giant as the space around us
                              our spirit vulnerable and desiring.

FROM RAWLINS TO ROCK SPRINGS

The face was impenetrable
I see it on the staring land

Flat   indifferent   rail hard
Mean   and whipped by the wind

Impersonal as a train
Hauling coal   across the Wyoming plain

I remember him   remember the face

Where the land forsakes
Like the abandonment of Icarus

When he fell out of the sky,
A long   forsaken cry

TO THE CREATURES OF GALAPAGOS

I have no claim to your territory
on these black lava-washed rocks
whose ancient fierce rising
is your floor.

I have not worn armor to your place
nor would I take one more step
into your proud tame gaze, strange kin,
in this splendid hour
unattached from violence anywhere.

And as surely
I breathe,
so do first forms
lie in pools,
systems evolving my beginning —
I am there in a single cell.

The waves explode geysers
over swirls of lava
over moss, out of mind with green,
equatorial stars curve fully
around the earth where you live.

Here, I am without a shadow . . .
Your gaze, eclectic creatures,
has made me gentle, with whispered steps.
I will remember, when I meet my enemy.

AUBADE – ASSISI

Birds in the cathedral are lifting dinosaurs
the morning cantilevers through the dawn
over the structure of the church.

Now the faces of three days
contemplate the sunrise
in the light of fine memory.
Given hands they would turn them over
and over
washing light and wheat,
sharing one coin.

And on the third day
a pure philosophy hums through the morning,
making a song over the fields.

When low red cars race
a noon inferno
slashing diagonals across the fields,
scarring a face

St. Francis of Assisi
holds the pain in silence,
in priceless redemption.

As We Make Our Legacies

LEGACY

Each night one drum hollows
the wolf-half moon
for the word to echo
year after year.

The air is spartan clear
cleaning the wind,
the echo rides . . .
weaving through caves, cities, portals, trees
wide
to where the earth curves — the color of orange.
It breathes where prayers turn to face the east
knees in the sand.

The word is decoration, silver festivals
bronze singing spears
holding it up.

The word is stretched with thong and sinew
around the earth.

One word makes an echo
in the hollow space of the moon.

One word lies in the throat
of the first native on earth.

It is so old, no one can name it
but I call it Song.

OLD MAN AT THE SEA

The breakers are collecting rhythm
To the beat of his heart
The sound is everything
In between nothing
That is not white and blue.
The old man whittles
Into the next century
Obeying canons in his head
Untangling fishnets
Imagining women in sprawling sand.
His permanent spirit grows wider
On the Greek shore
On out —
On the Aegean Sea.

THE FAMILY NAME

The families pass
Like swift migrations
Century after century
And lie down wearing granite
And marble
Their ghost steps — coins in the leaves
In the valued woods
As we press our reverence on a chain
Toward their marks left there
Wearing the links
Like a crown.

ARTHUR COMES TO THE NURSING HOME

Unrelenting shuffle in the half-light
Their thoughts in mauve
To match the violets
Limp in the indoor window sun
Shuffling through valleys of halls
Their eyes never open to stars
The age of these women
Was stacked, put away.

One day an old man came,
Old Zeus
Taking regal strides
Like a Legionnaire
Curious as a gnarl.

The equilibrium of his eyes
Leveled their minds.

It seemed to them
He threw them garlands from a story
And they gave him sketches of smiles
Darting like birds through a cage;
The days were more now
Than just threads dragging through sand.

But as the sun turned mauve
Arthur shuffled through valleys of halls
. . . a thread dragged through sand . .
Nothing more.

RURAL ESCAPE

Each day of summer
As long as fifty years
A child in her was picking berries
In the ring of the air of morning,
Placing them one by one
From the bush with wet beads
Into a pail,
Small ringing
Not far from the waist

A classic thing.

Far from the afternoon packed in heat
With vines lying down
Tangled in her heart

While the distance of evening
Waited
A soothing
Spread low and cool
On the turn of the earth.

DAILY RITUAL

My Grandfather never went there
where pilings howled with dissension of old men
there on that wharf in Long Beach
dwarfed by oil derricks, reserved for the Spit and Argue
    Club (it must have been 1936 or so)
though it might be supposed
he might like to have,
to be able to aim far into the water
instead of a homemade spittoon.

But he didn't chew
or argue
wringing brown flavor from a plug.
He had a cigar, he smoked like a king each day
put out of the house by his wife
to the garage or back lawn chair.

Probably the only abstractions he ever made
were in the perfect rings he blew
mouth in an O
gazing them into slow moving, disappearing shapes
like surrealistic dreams.

When the cigar had been savored
when thumb and forefinger almost met
he stood up
his spine piercing a straight line
shoulders thrown back to be rid of blades,
then he took a walk
thinking about the world news
reaffirming convictions
getting ready for the night
with only a hint of paranoia
when he propped chairs against the doors
in case the Russians came.

SCHEMA

Wood splinters the far light
Cracking open the fall.
Summer had been braided
With the full scent of bodies,
Water and salt
Wild on the dunes
Color flying on the hills
Sweet and bitter as a cut.

A glossary now   terms of love let go
Seen with an elusive eye
That tries to forget
That three month life,
Brought up brittle
In the autumn chill
An edge of pain   so poignant
Sweet and bitter as a cut.

That summer is caught on an echo
Of wood that splinters far light,
An echo that is new and ageless old
Carries memories to frost
In the stinging chill.

MINE SHAFT

Better understand
that life here is metal
determined women, hard at the elbow
who know the tooth of the mountain
lights the surface
of their man's brain . .

pulls them underneath
like dark lions.
Something almighty heavy
from the long line of their fathers
takes them there
or maybe the incessant flicker of fool's gold
trapped in a corner of their minds.

The women see from various windows
the tailings pond — testimony
to the strand of hair
that falls in their eyes.
They should get something
from the counters they polish
like silver slivers, gold dust — something unreal
a cerulean surface
like a nice day at the end of the tunnel
that they slant toward.

CENTER OF THE ORDER

Nuns with cool meditations
cool as the moon on platinum waves
rise early
spread the morning out on a white cloth
unattached to the passionate color
of the dawn.

Nuns gather at the center of the day
away from the noon's hot disc:
under Romanesque arcades
they have cool meditations
in the shade.

Often in the evening
they stroll from the Convent,
to stand beside the sea, habits flying
centered in the circular calls of gulls,
gulls winging in blood-red sun
over swollen waves.

Sea winds move onto land
Nuns stand motionless in the center of the wind
their minds,
like the eye of a storm.

WHO IS THIS EARTH

It is the strong color of ancestors
that strikes your high angular face,
proud and windowless as the Inca
powering through these blocks of stone.
With that same strength
you set your feet
one before the other,
stepping on echoes
each step an indissoluble print
locking into your puzzle
that is forever searched by the lost,
the ornamental.
You, Indian,
are unquestionable as all seasons
all cycles
steady as the hat
that you wear
in these tall Peruvian Andes.

DIADEM: END OF A SEASON

The harbor is closed in winter sound
Empty to the sounding deep
Delights of sea-side flowers pressing now
In pages of a book.
And there are prints
Twice upon the shore
Going on and out of sight — totally dissolved.
Such flights out to the edge
That late summer brings.

The summer sky with gulls
Is solid now to freeze
No feasts from boats
Horn them down.
One imagines in cold crystal fantasy
Siren calls or Ithaca and Odyssey.

In bare defense
We cling to a last and latest leaf
Gathered way up beyond the shore
Conceding then, throw it as a token
Upon the water
Winter deep.

EXTRAPOLATION

a boy kicks a rural stone along the road
    in late afternoon
    the road stares
time is a white lake — a metronome
    each century a hand waves
    hardly noticeable
dust rises from the road
    fragile in late sun
    historically gold
the same sun — a bronze Roman disc
    slants across the stones
    on the Appian Way
time is hollow forever
    the sound of the stone falls in
the boy goes on . . probably deaf

RESURRECTION OF A HERO

Ships carrying new men
ply toward you, Cú Chulainn
rude interferences, challenging your name.
You pay no attention,
as if you could man the sea
anytime
there in a wild mist
strong as Gaelic script, Irish God of the Sun.
Hands on hips
astride the sea
you seem taken with old Gaelic ways
tying green ribbons
to exclusive language:
You, Irish God of the Sun
resurrect the breed of old national spirits,
not letting a shipload of brogue
keelhaul your lines of Gaelic words.

IN COMPANY WITH IMPRESSIONISTS

". . . Oh be crazed for the fire in which something boasting with change is recalled from you; that designing spirit, the earthly's master, loves nothing as much as the turning point of the soaring symbol."

— Rainer Maria Rilke

It is the innocence of the Renoir face
the ease   detachment
that is the deceit of art.

The turning point of the soaring symbol
the fire of change
is a demon
driving to the edge.

Pissarro vibrates
shimmering in oil and sun
green light singing in the atmosphere
to Rilke's demon-angels.

La Mer or the Water Lilies of Monet
we stretch to parallel.
The demon though   it is the demon
that must cross the fine line of risk
that genius sharpens with a knife . . .

van Gogh bleeding in the thickness of his paint
where the angel lives.

THE HORSEMAN

Driving around the curve of a hill
that day
it came to mind — something like
North to Cumberland,
the slow motion of a horse running
a man leaning into the hill — riding
all golden in the afternoon sun
as if it might be Wordsworth with the reins
trailing rags of Napoleonic Wars
pages of Blake rustling in one hand
high in the air.
Now the sun is melting him into the hill
that lies like a lamb.
Perhaps tonight a full moon
will gather reason into mellow light
shining on the lakes of Cumberland;
forests and streams will sign
a fresh new century.

THOSE PLAIN PEOPLE

This is poor land
There is plowing
The sun into the moon
With dust

Stars measure receded dreams
From a sky that cantilevers incessantly
Not giving rain

Yet it is here they home
Minds still
Sure as geometry
A straight line going on and on
Beyond a point

From old histories
They hold up the earth

"What is it they have,"
We say

WITHIN A FRAME

strings in the garden, the harpsichord
a touch of Fragonard
the garden wings, singing,
slippers of rose on needlepoint
a vase, one bud
fragile as a Watteau painting

penned messages
secrets of Cocteau
planned arrangements of Versailles
lie dormant in her,
sitting by the window
winding lace
viewing spring
face
as blank as burial

BLIND DREAM

She kicked one stiff rotten peel.
The only color on that one-way street
Was phosphorescent flies
Excited by excrement.
She was bombed before she began
Laid into the trap.

What fair is there
The tube
Tells her she can
Go off swinging soft pearls and sun
And grow seashells in her hair
And that she
Should wait as proud and graceful
As a swan.

HARD, TOUGH LADY

Twisting the outer shield
all the gloss and semi-gloss
on a wall gone dry and parched
and marginal
everything is presently cracked
moments
lying tough
embossed with freighted permanence
on the steaming street

to the porch where she sat.

In this layer
under this layer
a body of thought — her thought
deep as a lake
nails a red branch
as it dips in the cool,
rich water of plenty
creating ripples across the fence.

She laid four words on the landscape
into the summer heat.
It was like a key turning
unlocking something human
something deep
I mean miles more
than summing up the weather.

Now Cora is dead. No.

From her raw, brazen, iron horizon
now in the heat
there is slight rain in gold light
gold mist . .

transcendence,
dissolving those dark institutions
of difference.

COMPUTER ROOM

We are etched like empty chairs
in green air
a dinosaurian landscape
non persona.

Pity,
we are surfaces
our pulse diluting through wires
and terminals,
screens of visual obsession.
Yes pity,
this glaze.

There are no notes on leaves, no windows
in the flat of this marginal room
nor a raw pitch and rant of the wind
no sun, no ancient textures, plumage
of myths.   No rare and rich works
no oeuvre.

SREBRENICAS

Surely
in the beginning
the light must have been quiet
throughout the world
the same breath in us all.

We used to enter the sound of breathing
as we walked in dusk,
color sifting from a red sky
like psalmists
entering some part of us
that was a song.

But now
the moon cries, scarred
looking down on mountains of skulls, staring
all honor   all spirit
shattered
like exploding, broken glass.

In the killing fields   in the craters of death
we run between fire
and black sun

easily   easily
we are viewed through gauze
pawns
drained into the system   dismissed
to politics of caprice
vanishing
soundless screams,
               history
without a face.

DETOUR: PERIOD PIECE

Each morning she dusted the platitudes
The ones that hung in the hall
The great marble entry
Took them and went out
Distributing them as dreamed primers of perfection
And the proper glaze for the occasion
In the elegance of stores.
Then lunch under a Manhattan cut glass chandelier
Four martinis later
Four o'clock in the afternoon
Got her barely to a taxicab.

Each day was prepared from a mold
Perhaps occasionally distilled
A shade off gray
Wearing pearls
Then the same route home to
Through the iron gates.

In her fever of monotony
The only fever she knew
She noticed this time,
Raking slightly the boredom
The taxi detoured

Down Delancy street
Cheap jar the color of round gum machines
That stared back at her — violent
Stinking and bold

God, she had never made a statement like that street.
Every night
Her quartets of dreamed things passed by.

GEORGIA O'KEEFFE

She takes it all and says, "here,

See."

I have this bone blue space
And I strike the sun
More vivid than it is.

It is.

My forms flow on
But go back
To that most essential place.

I am.

The moon hung sharper
Framed in clouds darker
Against lights brighter

Because that night
I saw O'Keeffe.

And because I saw
The day was total orange
Slashed round in red

The next night
Was electrified
With a pin of light
Way back on a flat
Total black
Sea

And the next day
Was flowing solid forms
Out and back to

Who I am

She takes it all and says, "here,

See."

IN REMEMBRANCE OF BATTLEFIELDS

Flowers had lifted the fields
Rolled them out to the edge
Peeled in the direction of all seas
We saw then
Underneath
The cranium of war

Flanders — Lidice — Vietnam impaled.

All those names had lifted too
Up toward the sun
Sounding a mantra.

The evening bleeds magenta

And this night
Under the direct stare of the moon
Megatons of white heat, clubs and guns
Send every soul
Into deeper graves of prehistoric form
Sounding along the nerve
Like strung gut
Tuned to the highest decibel.

Each ghost calls its name
To the next mark on the grave;
Crossed rows in fields
Covered with flowers

And we are very afraid.

STOCKBROKER

you are a
thoroughbred
running on a
blue wire
cool
as the moon
a managed fortune
with all
its disciplines
in hand
you sizzle
through
the white hot
perimeter
through
frenzied tape
with
that cool look
on your face
you see
the
blue gut
of
the wino
lying in the street
you see
with no
compassion
through
your
sparkling
glass of
luncheon wine
the one
that
makes your
day

your steps
springing out
of the rags
of him
out of
the glass
it is not too
late
to lose
a fortune

RADICAL ACTS

The bus gears through a tunnel
a tomb of monochromatic.
I am monochromatic, going under the river
leaving the establishment on the other side.
Beyond now   a bruised sky
raw tenements increasing
blocks of weeds — trash among them
some kind of beige finality.

It is not tempered,
this delivery of unfortunate scenes
only that a little gold leaf
is peeling from the side where I live.

A long street
a jagged rake   iron grates
a retch
there is no hum of roses
for those outside the windows of the bus.

A long street
paved with unhinged lives.
Incredulous
a gentleman stands at the end
white   apparitional   tall
reaching into his own praise,
offering to be Adonis or Godot.
Now we see through the glass darkly,
they wasted him without a breath
blew him away
put a bullet in his head.
It isn't anything,   déjà vu
a little river of scarlet on the street.

And so I think it takes a long time
going up long spiral stairs out of this

like trees that stand and wave forever
till you recognize pure sound
and the buoyancy of light articulates.

Now I would like to go far away and
see something pure Gothic
like the soaring frames of light
through the windows of Sainte-Chapelle

and then perhaps get off the bus
on their side
offering nothing.

LEVELS OF PREJUDICE

It is a strong Brown River
rude,
it is dull freight
it is fine silk mud —
storm clouds assemble here
gathering their brutal history.

Cars stream beside the River
like blue and red wind
like exploding stars,
a large white hand
is mixing the psyches of millions
throwing them into buildings.
They are like statues with velocity.

Inside,
marble walls mirror perfect
"urban plan" city trees
there is passing comfort in these leaves.

The marble is just a little high
to reflect the River
the value of fine silk mud is hidden —
continuing a flat surface

continuing business
as usual.

ISOLATION

It is more fortunate than we thought
this place inside time (as we would have it)
the repetitious sounds not crossing
therefore believable
like the ringing of one bell
the sound clear and correct
and these exquisite pulsating lines
electric
bright with desire   the privilege of this

    and we see the smooth way people walk
    on the other side of the window
    (because it is glass).

And now we are revolving through a glass door.

Does it bother us really
the exhibit in this museum of art
people folding in photographs
inside their bruised, nude bodies
looking out of great shadowed eyes
without desire
nothing in the empty high baroque halls

    souls more hollow
    more starved than desire,
    supreme edge of the mad
                                        lunacy.

We are redeemed however
when we leave
and glimpse a face on the corner
a young man in late winter sun
his head like Phoenician gold

    reminding us somehow
    of Vienna   resounding in us
    in golden tones   that place

when we were there   with the privilege
of wandering filled baroque halls
clothed and warm
in awe   and satisfied

reminding us
                        only
it was so long ago.

PROGRAMS IN THE EVENING OF CHILDHOOD

A flow of connected lives
Wheels slowly through front rows
Through field days and ribbons,
Platforms of off-key
But honorable sound
To patriotic parental faces
Whose eyes seize in a glance
Say — that's my child.

This flow of connected lives
Wheels slowly through front rows
Measured in school.

A program is floating
In long dresses white shirts
Tears in April and May
As we hug the child's years
Wreathed in daisies
That will lie soon on the shadow length
Of slanted sun
In the evening of childhood school.

This flow of connected lives
Wheels slowly from front rows.
Tears may dry in June
Return again
When there is that echo
That familiar tune from childhood
Measured in school.

All These Interiors

INTERIOR

PART I

Here now
at this first moment
at this first glance
there is no interior in the view

no crescendo
I am busy driving the highway
under the bridge.

I recall over and over
a man walking across
in the morning mist of an unfinished winter
walking over a stream of sound   cars underneath
walking into the formless pale of winter
walking into reality   the mundane

as on an invisible wire   slow ghost thing
going on forever   inexorable.

I recall now
the view
the man walking
attached and detached
turning, not considered

here now
this then
became my interior

a measurement
point on a wire
attached   detached
walking directly into the mist
calling
walking into reality   the mundane

here now.

PART 2

I felt a dangerous effort
breaking below the earth
disparate, hard, fractured
and many parts of darkness,
a whole history of silent accuracy
in her face

this crippled woman   mute
the muted space between us
a compelling, contextual question there
and I was reduced to cambrian stone.

The question owns me
it lives in the shadow of light
lives in a fifth season
where I have not arrived

the question becomes a monogram
in many mirrors   yet
escapes me.

It is becoming myself   my interior
a larger search

it is all the fortune
that I can stand.

Part 3

around the lake
so many years around
the smooth glass water
the buried deep
among the interims I have missed
I have missed the willow tree
the man with the limp
these proclivities
how they persevere
engaging
the nature of all things

the subtle drop of the branch to the water
long lending its arch to the lake
magic as the Golden Bough

then again, the mouth so grim
the man with the cane
each day   daily walks with a limp
the time he smiled
was into a shadow
as if the shadow might steal it away

the tree   the man   the water
the bough   the smile   the lake sublime

the interior of me.

Part 4

Then in the presence of one fine day
this finest day
no honor greater
than swimming toward each other
the water smooth, perfect, accepting
    gliding together
as if the universe had meant it
all along.

While you were formed
I waited
with each breath
    yours and mine
yours within you, quite apart from mine
yet the rhythm one.

Your imprint from the past
is yours alone
    will print
beyond the frame of time
this, the most exciting thing
this new person I will meet
to join, you, who are already,
my interior child.

Look everyone, see our children
how each child lifts us
    a child angel of Donatello.

STANDSTILL

A stone turns in the length of a sun's years.

My heart turns to measure the light
that rushes by through glass.
    I look out to find those fine sensibilities
    trees — flowers, going by too fast
    but see only the reflection of my face.

I wish to reach out and touch
the fire of growing, in my fingertips
    fire of color, gathered in bunches;
    to throw it, shout, run through it,
    bathe in it, sing.
    I would offer all this color to the nameless.

Now I will try to lie down and look at a flower,
in a sun that is fragile and compassionate.
    I will lie down under trees
    on this enormous circumference;
    lie down where I can see the design of the seed,
    try to see myself in it.

I will break the glass
before I see autumn leaves lying as a wake
    and will offer all of myself
    to an eventual nameless design.

And then I will get up.

TRIBUTARIES

She took me down there
My daughter,
Down the mountain
Weaving wild paths
To her places — nooks
Made secret
In the delicate corners of her mind.
And I savored this shared honor
Washed in spring water
Slipping into each small place
She had gathered
For the history of this spring.

Down to the brooks
To the stones — the glass water
Smooth as the cool
Of my daughter's mind,
Around each bend.

See this — see this!
Which do you like best?

The moss and three flowers
Claiming five wet stones
With sound, quiet as slips,
Or where flowers in miniature
Break crags like rococo
Shouting the spring away?

She contemplated each scene
Clear and long — giving it to me,
Smoothing the stones over hundreds of years.
And we flowed like rivulets
Each which way, into confluence
Into long memory

She was weaving a spring
A montage.

CINQUAIN
(Iron Son of Russia)

Below

on the Neva

a Russian fisherman

holds his world on his red striped shirt

broad back

The War

Memorial

above the river bank

loads the air between line and fish

Iron Son

My son

wants to take a

picture because he's

crazy over fish   the same, the

world over

TRANSPARENCY

This morning I took some distance
crystalline — untenable
and spread it across my palm
for our son.
The light was trembling
pure as the river I run beside
washing the air
washing through me
and the whole full yellow of autumn
told me the time was right.

Now he can form the air
I told him
the way he pleases.
Now everything seemed honorable
as he is honorable
as is his search for ancient marks
as trees are always honorable
and all the extravagance
of heroes and legends of sons
slanted in.

I have been in a corner
in a thin edge of the moon
on a thin branch — fragile
waiting for the nest to unwind.

This morning I saw the clouds part and roll off
in the shapes of the hills they covered;
I could see then in the sky
the clear blue of his eyes
as I passed myself going — a transparency,
child that I am
on the way.

SOMETHING ABOUT COLLISION

These children are full of lights and comprehensions
they can't articulate
    they are deep in parental folds.
These layers of gold leaf we mold on them
are heavy.
    The next day parents are not noon suns
    we are low on the horizon.
    It is where inside, the children reside
    where we
    reside   that is the difference.
It is where my daughter resides now
that is deep value
    intelligent tides pulling her;
she is gold without me   has always been.
And when she is in the sound of being alone
    let it be like shells filling with light.
Sometimes
when she leaves the door open
it is nice that these rooms are tinged with a breeze
    more light please
    more light
    so I can see   can respect her thin shell,
    how delicate it is.

THE POOR ARE OFTEN SILENT

hearts in rows of little windows
faces
like pieces of string hanging, saying nothing
closer to the street each day
as cars dive past
melting into the highway
one block away
past their little patches of green
in front
as if someone had stuck them on
with a thumb
turning more yellow from fumes each day

every house must have — has a small light

and the porches are nice
when the relative comes over
sits — says nothing
grows one day older on the family vine
shares bread each day
and on the holiday
with three colored bulbs in the windows
shares candy, canned meat and beer
and one more year
the houses show lime green under pink
the porches are peeling but still holding
the relative who is eighty five
protected if need be
with knives   enough
to put lives on the line.

THERE IS A SOUL HERE

Air moves through corridors of bamboo
as if transparent hands
were waving smooth green light . . .
the least imperfect noise
would ruin the culms' hollow sound
the least name whispers on the air
this is where the place inside
is its own groaning, creaking song.
It is perfect singing;
a choir, in the giant green.

SHOAH

There is little to say
that I can say
little to stand on.
Every day I give myself
absolution
turn from blue shadows
into sun
let the wind arouse me
behind shelter
sweat in the sun
it is not much   easy expenditures.
I fly to the water
the aquamarine water
and white sand
to escape seeing
the barren orchard.
But now
all my life   from now on
I will hear those trains
going to the ovens   boxcars of bodies
the beat of those train wheels on rails
on the tracks.

ANOTHER MOCK-UP

It is a large moon
on a long industrial shore
this shore
something monstrous but proud about it.

It is midnight
and the bridge is a roof over rags
each life under, empty as the moon
blank as the moon
each life meant to shine
and the guts of the matter is
not romantic.

Picking a way among feathers
is easier than this.
Brother with sister, I can't see you
but a longshoreman's shout
is nothing
beside your cry
frozen in dirt.

CAUSEWAY

for Pat Lewis

The sum of your endurances
the hard invisible stone of it
the farthest sight
looking out over empty seats at night
alone
in a stadium of white walls
(blank token acceptances of this decade).
Add it up
the sum of your Black endurances
I mean the pain of the
hard invisible stone of it.

When you face me
it is a matter of routine   your survival
tough travels for you and your kin.

Every waking hour you must sift the white words
so they will blow away more easily
blow away before they cover you

and for your children
you haze narrow perimeters
haze the hard line in colors
most visible to hope
though it has never been thought a possibility
judging from all those conversations
used over and over   audible
inside the white walls.

However it turns out for you
it turns on a wheel of heroics
you cross over

inside your dark velvet skin   all one
not broken
unbroken
total
surely it is shining.

WHATEVER IS THE NAME
(Time With Ashbery)

. . . on the other side of 5:00 A.M.
no numbers   it is less than
a flat place, just beyond
the end of a game   before luminosity
before the opiate sun   before shadows
so that coming and going are the same
and directionless
and flat   stones take a flat stance   naturally
a flat heart

if we realized — we would be bored
like being in a museum too long
in Dali too long
spread out in all that twisted space
too much activity there and
no energy for it   just limitless
    nothing coherent

given another hour maybe
a fresh order
the air will be like excerpts from Bach   light
and flying
bouncing against outrage   accumulations
acquisitions that come with the process of day
meanwhile on the other side of 5:00 A.M.
there are no corners
a cover of velvet
    nothing surgical

we will be honed in the light of day
but now is nothing with the exception, that
we breathe,
so stunning a process
being the bones of a sustained song
    it is astonishing
in this value between
lies zero — we are a part   though nothing here

is divisible   it is so divisible
no chromatics   just monotone
we are leveled   shelved
no flags   with nothing to sound
under the dome

if there were a dream   it would be flat
like the planes
of an industrial building
      at night
seen from a black highway
across a field   with one light affixed
      stark on the building
shining in a triangle on the surface
reminding one of the non-function
of functional things   that lonely quality

delicate connection

if all hearts were lined
      with the patterns of this seashell
            almost perfect, more delicate than lace

there would be no war

for we would contemplate
      the sensitivity
            of our hearts

how the lines
      are the same motion as the design
            on the shell

you see this shell
      is the shape of a heart,
            like fine porcelain, is translucent

so there is shadow
      the shadow behind   the shadow behind
            our hearts as well

shall we move this seashell through our hands
      this dynamic
            this intrinsic reflection

TO THICH NHAT HANH

These stalks   these pods that rattle,
remind me of the bamboo of your country

but what particular thread unwinds
among the brittle autumn pods
to show me why the importance of your footfall
the sound of its shape,
strikes my mind with silence.

Today
this dust-gold haze of autumn
is the blood-brown haze
from the burning of your country.
And you, in your brown robe
walk through,
stronger than lions
in your silence.

The way you use the air
the shape the air gives you
is your breath forever,
. . clear and artesian
and I,
from the west
don't know when to be silent.

AUTUMN CAMEO

Silence — oh yes, the silence was rust
that early morning I ran through haze.
I ran through vapor,
chilled by wet
rust-red leaves.
The haze, the vapor swirled
I almost disappeared

as if an oracle would steam and rise
distilling magic through a copper sun.

Ahead, I saw a rust-red dog
I almost heard a bugle
almost saw the hunting coats of red:
the dog's coat was flowing like the hair of Venus,
wave upon wave
and wave upon wave of other autumns swept me
deep into leaves, complexities   each year a mirror.

Actually, the dog was stretching up,
along the grains of bark
looking for a squirrel.
It was simple as an Aesop fable,
a tree — a dog — a squirrel
it was primeval.

IDENTITY

It is in the sound of wings
beating at silence
vaulting the cathedral
in purple light

and out of tragedy,
a bird singing
breaking through crystal
to that singular sound

when I know myself
deeper than bone.

And the wind,
a fierce erasure,
carves who I am.

Through the long line of time
seeing a dolphin
swimming in lineal, exotic identity
its elliptical signature a paradigm,
its eye is wiser than mine.

In columns
through columns of pillars
these libraries, heroic temples
through tall French, Italian trees
in this countryside
through the gnarled Greek Olives
lies everything, becoming something
as I walk there.

I stand on the cliff
near a lighthouse, breaking time
above this polarity where currents oppose,
Pacific and Tasman Seas
I am juxtaposed
a venue of angular perceptions
pulled and slanted by waves

recalling wave after wave
of human complexities, in cities
relentlessly near.

I wish, simply
to place my fingers on the shadow of a branch
in the sun
till each finger becomes a branch
singularly
till my hand is absorbed into the tree.

This Eucharist sears;
a brand on my memory,
not to be forgotten
in a world eclipsed by terror
but after all
a turning, brilliant arrangement

that we go into every day.

ANOTHER REALITY

Among shadows of leaves
The sun diffuses all names
One year meets all others
In this pacific quiet.

The leaves brush my memory
In the same tone
As they brush the sun
On the white wall
As if quiet had come forever.

Absorbed into definition
Thin as illusion
I do not wish to look outside the window
To see the tree   the sun.

Not chained in Plato's cave
I choose these inside shadows
To move across my mind
A parable of reality.

This late afternoon on the wall
Like a perfect lawn of low sun
And shade
Like first toys lying down,
Silent
In the long memory that rests me
As if it could be forever.

I am young and old and everything
And nothing
In this mellow afternoon
Of summer.

THE OCCASION

Two birds flying low
A piece of paper blows
An old man bends against the wind
Up the street of a mountain town
Usually a tourist swarm
Empty as a hull this day
of my 49th birthday.

In the city that night
Dressed for the occasion,
(ever so slightly)
We walked up stairs
To swing with lines in pictures
Be absorbed with the painted people
Moving like an amoeba to protect their drinks
Gliding and glancing into art
People watching over the undercurrent
Of conversation — as if they were being filmed
then back down the stairs
of this historic restoration
In old downtown.

Into the car past a corner
Where a piece of paper blew and an old man
Bent
Held his hat against the wind
Waiting for a bus

Sliding up into mirrors
And chandelier lights
A penthouse restaurant
Surrounded by waiters
Smooth on the music with hardly a beat
Eating money that tasted good
drinking cocktails instead of drinks
Moving together in a dance then gliding down
Back to the car in the wind
Thinking about the two old men

And pieces of paper
And next year I'll be 50 —
I'm rude to myself and think
So what.

A MEMORY
(Reflections From Noguchi)

Snow is falling on the river
As I reach through this stone
To a portrait
Invisibly there
Even softer than melting
Silent
This silence
Older than gods
It is, as the stone is silent
But stones don't melt . . .
I turn away
Taking back the stone
Go ahead pressing wet leaves
To the pavement
Now one breath precedes my own
I catch up
It is yours   is with me
We lie silent as the snow
Falling on the river

WEDDING ON THE HIGH EDGE

Let all these elements combine
columbine   utterances of all these flowers

these wild flowers
against the tall ecclesiastical mountain

and the breeze
the clarity of this breeze

shapes each word like a bell
in the fine aerial morning

shapes into vows
ordained by a summer day.

Be one
in flowers, words, blue, trees, sun

your promises heralding
across the valley

are carried on the color of wild flowers
each one reaching up on the note of a flute

high in the granite
of the Mount of the Holy Cross   till it sings.

May each promise honor the flowers' return
year after year

and the constant power
of the mountain

this day   old as myth   purest laurel,
bonds, wreathes your universe

as the breeze lifts through the veil,
through the white mist

flows through you as you walk,
linking arms

up and on and over a hill,
you are filtering the sun.

JAZZ AND ALL THAT . . .

rock   beat
fills all this space
crucifies the air

I feel like vapor   smoke and fuchsia
jazz and all this   heat
hot notes
the beat   is   coming on

through a glass of scotch

the beat is in the room
is in the room inside
the room is going on

the beat is going on

I am flowing in the
mindless liquid in the room
we are all one mind   the
mindless sliding notes

the soldiers are going now
moving the big machine
the round political machine

its machinations
moving over the scarlet bodies
of us all.

SONG WITHOUT WORDS

That I could touch you
That I could say it
As petals fall, breathing the ground tender
That I could say it that way
In the blue silence of the sky
Reaching out to worlds asleep,
That I could say it
So silent
Bells shatter to crystal
Breaking open more space between,
That I could say it as a whisper
Reaching a flower turned to seed
That on the breath floats in the air
Forever,
That I could say it
So light it brushes trembling
Like the value of a note
That lasts into silence
And makes the silence another song
Another way.

AT THE CENTER

For one instant
the shadow of the wings
the long jet hung
suspended
in the sun
straight across the spectrum
I saw Dantean circles
blinding in the center

therefore the plane was placed
into the origin
we were riding in the origin
of the shadow
the eye startled
by violet green energy
in the center of the Epic
as in a mirror

the Medici would pay well
for this one perfection

then the speed of the jet
sliced us out of the circle
and the plane's shadow lay back
on the great comfortable lap
of the clouds.

IT IS WHEN YOU SAY MY NAME

You speak one word
It is my name.
The way you say it
Rings like an ancient blossom
That is said on the branch of Tao-chi.
It rests there in the quiet
Like ancient Chinese
It rests on the stream between two mountains
That flows forward in all time.
And we see that we are written forever
Your word upon me is old
It is a seal   it is Our name.

SYMBIOSIS

All around is dull
trees   fields   brush.
It is almost expected
(because you read a Russian novel
saw a Bergman film)
that smoke or haze
will rise slowly through the scene
the flavor of some large industrial movement
underneath
as the catalyst
as in marshes too
(you have seen on film, in paintings)
the mist.

Inside yourself
driving into the facts
winter is dull as cold without snow
haze of carbon monoxide lingers,
turns brown in lungs.

We think there should be a light
that smiles forever.
The magazines tell us
to go get a package of stars
drink them for breakfast   think them
wear one on a sleeve
put them in the trees for leaves
pull yourself off
this dull course.

But in the symbiosis with winter
you know what you really are.

THE EARTH HAS SUCH STYLE

I am set in motion
viewing the tall grass
moving air

my roots
are interlaced
in its biologies.

Though I wish for such grace
as the winning flights of birds
and the way the tall grass
moves,

I burn like a violent face
as I step on these systems,
a great clod

covering with dirt —
balances, reliances
acoustical murmurings
layer on layer

I cover the delicate brain
of the earth.

RETURN

As sheets of wind
                    barely ruffle the water

an absentee bird sings
the soundless quality   audibly instructive
                    white sound

against these rocks   in the lake
these monumental metaphors
                    like the face of Yeats

serious as stone
                    and not unbecoming.

Through these woods
the damp and dark and shadowy days,
                    through the hollow tower

resonates his coming   his return to this place
of hazelwood and berry   and the green air suns
                    through clouds

the landscape   the water and the Isle
in the gnarled roots of home.

                    A great bird is tearing
                    our terrible indifference.

WHERE SHALL WE ALL MEET

Shall we go knocking on the sun
Dressed in jade and jewels
From this place
Barren as a stone
Thrown to the Dead Sea?

What did they mean
High up
The scribes of the Qumran
Who left us words
Lifted out of salt?

Or shall we fly
To the moon
To its great round
Into the very center
Untie ourselves
From the lumbering barge on earth
— the last wave?

What was meant at Sarnath
And under the Bo tree?

Perhaps a cry
Winding through an old shell
On this earth's shore
Is mending us
With some eternal mystic eye.

SPIRIT

It was never more clear
the light passing through this transparency

life, you know
wheeled out onto the tarmac

in the final analysis
drifting.

These moments before the fact   days
oh, they turn you inside out

place an order for
nothing

you are a window, you are
the Shelleyan fragility of leaves

shaking in the sun
you are the leaves.

This life to me
is here

in this ordinary
very ordinary placement of things to do

sculpting each movement   each moment
to the contour of the earth

where it is quiet
as an animal's spirit   is the flower's spirit

is ours. Your smile is ambient
taking care of space

the air is mellow.

WHERE IS INNOCENCE
(Eliot's Path)

All the words, the languid smoke
the language, eloquence
ennui
yet scattered within this intellect,
anxieties nettle
beneath long drinks on the lawn
beside the tennis court
and summer sails and sea.

Among the perfect blades of grass
fretted complexities
scatter like weeds
(landscape of the broken and disenchanted).

Smoke curls through discourse,
(the heart, disdained),
smoke fills the space
where the soul says,
Come here
before it is too late.

It is simple,
Come here
from outside the circle where you are
onto the round edge
the end and beginning and time suspends.

Now you see the flame in the center
silent   eternal
as you kneel, as you pray,
out of agony
out of dark.

THE INVISIBLE SEASON

Perhaps the seed is carried
      on a dark wing
perhaps it is still flying
perhaps it has fallen
      in a hidden place
perhaps before it is found
      it will be picked up
      and carried
on a black wing
      or a black, red and white wing
to a place that is brown,
      green and becomes all colors
      or no color
that we cannot see from here.

We won't know till we are there
      because it is between everything
      we now know
perhaps it will vanish even then
      but when we arrive
we will know it was here
      and we will go on from there
not looking.

Perhaps then
      it will be another season
too bright, too astounding to see
      but we will be certain   will know
it is there.

EVERY SO OFTEN

Something fresh is needed
Fair, fragile as Dresden
A first leaf, trembling
An occasional petal
Fragment of sun
Touching a mind
With the littlest word
For the first time.

ABOUT THE AUTHOR

Nancy Andrews has a previous collection of poetry, *Dimensions* (Graphic Impressions, Inc.), and her work has appeared in numerous periodicals. She is the editor-publisher of James Andrews & Co., Publishing. Poetry involvements have included participation in schools, poetry workshops at a youth correctional facility, and as coordinator of various community poetry events. She was educated at Stephens and Lindenwood Colleges and resides in Golden, Colorado, with her husband. They have two grown children, Bradford and Karen.